Alibertis

Follow us

In the GORGE of
SAMARIA

*A world of Nature, Life,
Legend and History*

Follow us
In the GORGE of SAMARIA

Central distribution: "Mystis"
Manouras Giorgios - Tsintaris Antonis Co.
Kalisperidon 15, Heraklion, Crete, Greece
Tel. 2810.226518, 346451
Fax: 2810.221908

Author: ***Alibertis Antonis, Grub-hunter***
Atalantis str. 12   71409 Agios Ioannis Crete Greece
Tel- Fax 2810323398

Photography: **Alibertis Antonis**
Cover: The third door
Back page: Synthesis of book photos

Lay out: Alibertis Antonis
English translation: Papadimitraki Maria

Printing: TYPOKRETA
Industrial Area of Heraklion, *Tel. 2810.380882*
e-mail : typokreta@her.forthnet.gr
www.kazanakis.gr

It is with love, devotion and respect
That I kneel before this miracle of Nature,
Before this unique landscape,
this Bulwark of liberty
Named SAMARIA.

Entrance to the gorge

3

Contents

Arrival at Xyloskalo early in the morning

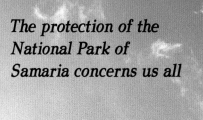

*The protection of the
National Park of
Samaria concerns us all*

Greece is among the most beautiful places of the globe.
Crete is one of Greece's most appealing places.
But no one questions that SAMARIA
is the most breathtaking place in Crete.

As the folk Cretan couplet (mandinada) goes:
"He, who hasn't seen the gorge of Samaria
and the plateau of Omalos
Hasn't really been to Crete."

Instructions for walkers in the gorge

The Samaria National Park is open to visitors from May 1st to October 31st, from 6 a.m. to 3 p.m. every day. Between 3 a. m and sunset visitors will be allowed only to the first two kilometers of the path from both entrances (Xyloskalo and Agia Roumeli).

Instructions for the visitors

Visitors are allowed to walk only on the main path (sign-posted) from Xyloskalo to Agia Roumeli and vice versa. Those wishing to walk along any of the other paths must have written permission from the Chania directorate of Forests and will be subjected to strict controls.

The following activities are strictly prohibited

Lighting fires. Camping. Overnight stays in the National Park. Picking up flowers. Uprooting or destroying plants. The removal or destruction of nests, eggs and fledglings. Destruction or damage to geological formations, signs and other property of the National Park and cultural monuments. Possession of weapons or traps. Dogs. Hunting and fishing in the National Park. Swimming in the streams.

The following activities are not permitted.

Radios. Singing. Throwing stones. Excessive noise. The disposal of rubbish in places other than those provided. Smoking except in the resting areas. The consumption of alcohol.

Protection Measures

The National Park is patrolled by forestry service rangers based at four locations inside the Park: Neroutsiko, Riza Sykias, Agios Nikolaos and Metamorfosi. There are fire faucets fully equipped and first aid kits. This equipment as well as the first aid kits are to be used by the visitors in case of fire or emergency and must not be destroyed. The village of Samaria has a phone for communication with the police in case of emergency, a drug-store, a heliport and two mules to transport those injured.

Penalties and fines

Those violating the above regulations will be persecuted and punished in accordance with articles 268, 275, 276, 277, 280, 285, 286 and 287 of the Presidential Decree 86/1969 "concerning the Forestry Code". The Rangers and the staff of the National Park are responsible for the enforcement of the above.

Chania directorate of Forests
Tel. 2810 22287

Entrance to the gorge is free for children until the age of fifteen and students with written permission from the forest authorities.

Useful tips

- Wear strong shoes and thick socks.
- Avoid carrying things with your hands. Use your back sack to carry your flask, some fruit or light food.
- Make sure to have at least one sandwich with you.

- Take your time to enjoy this magnificent gem of Nature.
- Don't put strain on yourselves and foremost do not rush down the great descent leading to the church of Agios Nikolaos.

First crossing of the river after the settlement

Some years ago, Antonis Skoulas, the legendary guardian of the gorge, while on duty at the exit guardhouse of Agia Roumeli, posed this question to the tired travelers:

"Well, fellows, what did you see in the gorge?"

"Nothing!" they responded.

"What do you mean?" he asked again.

"We were looking down the whole time, you see, being afraid of stumbling over a stone!"

7

Third door

White peony (Paeonia clusii)

What is Samaria?

Is it a magnificent landscape? A fathomless gorge? A perilous and yet sheltered path? An endless, still beneficial journey? A dream-like forest? The imposing peaks of the surrounding mountains that close in circle around it, called Madares? Or the impressive "gates?" Samaria is, in fact, all that and much more.

It is the thrill that comes from the forest, the unique fauna and flora, the charming waters and springs, the wind's fresh blow rushing through the "gates". The crossroad of history and legend. The unique place where today and tomorrow meet. But also fatigue and audacity. Force and pride. Desire, love and fulfillment. Adventure and discovery. Relaxation and ecstasy. A way to communicate with Mother Nature and one's self. This astonishing beauty strikes cords of the heart that were long forgotten.

Guardian's house - Entrance

9

The gorge of Samaria, familiar
Yet in many ways unknown

Most of the travelers that cross the Gorge of Samaria can't wait to reach Agia Roumeli. Only those accompanied by a guide and the experienced travelers have the luxury and time to appreciate the beauty of this gem of Nature which is the greatest and perhaps most beautiful gorge all over Europe. What about the vast majority of travelers?

Is it the fatigue? One's feet that start to stumble? Or is it one's yearning to get rid of the uncomfortable shoes as soon as possible? Maybe it is one's obsession to reach the end of the journey or the need to sink one's tired feet in the cold water? The desperate need to escape from the intolerable heat or the reflection of a cold beer together with the appeal of the mesmerizing and seductive sea? The fact remains these more than 2000 people who cross the gorge every day give the impression of being in haste.

Third door

The present guide will attempt to urge the restless visitor to get a better view of the gorge, appreciate things that he would have otherwise missed, indulge his curiosity, as well as entertain him and cause him to become fond of the gorge and – why not? – live for a while in this world of fairy-tales, history and legend, leaving the 16 km journey in the back seat.

Orientation

We are at the entrance of Farangas, the name given to the Gorge by the people of Sfakia, which also known as **Xyloskalo**. On this very rock shepherds have once used tree trunks and wood to construct some steps to unable their entrance in the gorge. Only the name of that construction has lived through the centuries. Some steps are curved in the rock.

We are surrounded by a magnificent landscape. The steep and rotten slopes of **Mt Gigilos** or Sapimenos (2086m), the mountain of Zeus, rise just in front of us. The legend has it that the king of the Gods used to move his thrown up there when he had enough of Olympus and the gods' disputes and intrigues. At the top of Gigilos, towards Omalos lies the natural platform, by the name of Agathoti, that Zeus was said to land his chariot.

The limestone guts of the mountain form impressive depths and mysterious caves that are inhibited by fairies, daemons, spirits, good or evil.

On our right, on the passage leading up to Gigilos, in the middle of an a vast scree, after the passage of **Xepiritas**, the arch made of huge rocks, the work of giants, we find the crystal waters of the **Spring Linoseli.** Its water is undoubtedly divine. Famous for its freshness, it is the coolest water in the island. The legend has it that Zeus used to bathe in these waters under the eyes of the nymphs that hid behind the rocks.

"Haunted tree"

Till this day the visitor who rests at the spring is able to hear their whispers and exclamations before the divine beauty! (The water that passes under the ground makes this whispering noise.)

The passageway, leading up to the mountain, begins at the pavi-

"Towers"

lion on our right. The winding path extends along the steep cliff which dominates the valley as far as Agios Nikolaos, passes from the towers and the spring, goes up the pass and reaches the top of Gigilos and Volakias (2.217 m.)

(Anchusa caespitosa) ✍

Tulip of Crete ⇨
(Tulipa cretica)

Berberis of Crete (Berberis cretica) ✍
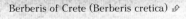

✍ Sainfoin of Sfakia
(Onobrychis sphaciotica)

Along this path one can encounter many endemic and rare plants as well as more common ones. Here are some of them.

On our left, a second pathway rises abruptly and leads to **Kallergis**. The Mountain Club of Chania has built the shelter of Kallergis at the edge of another cliff, which dominates the valley of Samaria. Having this shelter as a starting point, one can explore the high peaks of Melidaou, Pachnes and Trocharis, on our far left, which include rare endemic and exceptional plants. It is in this area and mainly in Poria (a natural pathway to Samaria) that we come across many bee-wives that feed exclusively on mountain flowers: thyme (Thymus capitatus), white thyme (Satureja spinosa), mountain tea (Sideritis syriaca), marjoram (Origanum microphyllum), savory (Satureja thymbra) etc. Their honey is delicious and the visitor can taste it in Omalos.

White thyme (Satureja spinosa)

Behind us the plateau of **Omalos** covers an area of 25 square kilometers, at an average altitude of 1080 m. above the level of the sea. Surrounded by high mountains it is almost always flooded during winter. The water forms beautiful ponds; especially in the south part which gradually drain away during summer. In the North, near the entrance of the plateau, just before the village, we encounter a great sinkhole, the cave of Tzanis or Honos that permits the flooded water to escape towards the valleys and the sea. French spelaeologists have explored more than 3km of subterranean galleries, reaching 600 meters in depth. The waters that flood the entrance of the cave cause a strange phenomenon: the air that is trapped inside this vast natural siphon tries to break free, creating huge bubbles that break causing the earth to shake as if a dynamite had exploded. The water that escapes reaches the hill as far as the carriageway.

This plateau, which gives the impression of being abandoned, used to be a source of life and wealth for the region. Wheat, barley, oat, potatoes, beans and other vegetables, known for their incredible taste once throve in these fertile grounds. Today, most of the land remains uncultivated and the visitor can only come across wild plants and flowers. Some of them, like the Sieber's crocus (Crocus sieberi) and the Baker's lily (Tulipa bakeri) are beautiful and bloom in the early spring.

Amassing of spiny chicory ⇨

16

zChurch of Saint Panteleimon ant tower of Chadzimichalis Yannaris, leader of 1896 Cretan Revolution

Other plants include the wild lettuce (Taraxarum bithynicum) in winter and the spiny chicory (Chicorium spinosum) in spring. These herbs, raw or boiled are delicious combined with lemon and oil.

Omalos has been the shelter of the Cretan rebels and was never conquered by the Turks. The plateau as well as the entire district of Sfakia remains a symbol of the endless yearning for freedom of the immortal Cretan soul.

Before beginning our descent we must dedicate a few words to Abelitsa (Zelkova abelicea). This is a unique tree that can only be encountered in the Himalayas. It belongs to a genus that was abundant in the North Hemisphere, at the beginning of the tertiary period, 65 million years ago. Today, there are only 4 species left, of which only one, Abelitsa, can be encountered in Europe.

It is encountered at 500 m. from the entrance of the Gorge. Shepherds used its wood to make the famous Cretan crooks or "katsounes".

Sieber's crocus
(Crocus sieberi)

18

Those who do not wish to visit the gorge should pay a visit to the **Museum of Natural History** that is next to the gift shop and snack bar and walk up to the pavilion to have a cup of coffee or grab a bite. The magnificent view is most rewarding!

The descent begins

We begin our descent at 1236m. We enter the word of fairytales and legend. The comparative photos try to show the difference between summer and winter. It is true that the winter snow and bad weather causes the gorge to appear imposing and frightening. One feels faced with invincible, supernatural and infernal forces: thick fog that seems to spring out of a boiling caldron, endless chaos and hollow sounds!

Mountain tea (Sideritis syriaca) ↘
↗ Scabius (Scabiosa albocinta)

Rock lettuce
(Petromarula pinnata) ⇩

A "female" cypress-tree (Cupressus sempervirens var. horizontalis) keeps us from losing our courage. It will keep us company until we reach the sea. Right in front of the guardian's house, we encounter a handful of mountain tea, the famous malotira, (Sideritis syriaca). Greek mountain tea is prepared from the dried flower-bearing stem of the plant and together with chamomile, pennyroyal, sage, marjoram and Cretan dittany, it is considered one of the most well known Cretan sippings.

Many chasmophytes can be found inside the rocks. A large number of plants find shelter in the gorge's and precipices' vertical slopes. The word "chasma" means abyss in Greek and it is in that abyss, between the often-vertical sides that we come across most of the endemic Cretan flora.

The visitor must be extra careful on the stone steps as they are worn out and thus very slippery and he should not be very confident with the wooden parapet as well, as the wood rots very quickly and the winter snow destroys the railing.

We then find ourselves at the lower side of Xyloskalo. The pathway is almost horizontal and is surrounded by the forest: Cypress trees (Cupressus sempervirens var.

Hooded cephalanthera (Cephalanthera cuculata) ⇨

Flax tree (Linum arboreum) ⍋

Lizard orchid of Samaria (Himantoglossum samariense) ⍋

horizontalis) but also pine-trees (Pinus brutia) maple trees (Acer sempervirens) kermes oaks (Quercus coc-cifera var. calliprinos) prickly junipers (Juniperus oxycedrus ssp. oxycedrus) and orchids: Cephalanthera cucullata, Himantoglossum samariense (see Wild orchids of Crete and Karpathos, author Antonis Alibertis)

23

On our right side and on our left, we leave two areas of retreat, ideal for those who want to get some rest or just savor the view, under the trees and the huge rocks.

Then, we pass in front of the entrance of a forbidden and dangerous pathway reaching the first spring, **"Neroutsiko"**. The water flows under a plane tree (Platanus orien-

talis). **We have crossed approximately 2 km**. The peach tree that the visitor discovers only a few meters away does not belong to the gorge's typical flora and it must be the result of a seed thrown by a careless visitor.

A short stop to freshen up and we find ourselves once more at the sideling pathway that leads to the bottom of the gorge. We are surrounded by the shadow of trees. A lot of them are pine trees. Pine trees were dedicated to Poseidon, the god of the sea because their flexible wood was, ideal to create the ships' flexible curves. Their resin was and continues to be, the main ingredient for the manufacture of the famous Greek retsina. Unfortunately pine trees are highly flammable. Beware thus! Do not throw anything in the forest! Even the smallest piece of glass can be proven dangerous!

Those of you who smoke should be patient until the next spring.

Unfortunately, the fire has long left its destructive marks on the area. Christophoro Buondelmonti mentions that in the 15th century a fire was burning the forests of the White Mountains for three entire years. Civran speaks of another fire that ravaged the forests of Sfakia for a whole year, in 1612.

We then move to reach the gorge's bottom. Our next stop is a around a small spring, called "**Riza tis sykias**" the "fig tree's root". On the rock's sides we find some mulleins (Verbascum arcturus) an endemic plant, which likes the shade.

Close to the food of Gigilos, a bit further of Linoseli stands the famous cave of "Demonospilios" the cave of Devil. It is said that it used to be Apollo's oracle. Another myth has it that a shepherd plays a demonic theme on his lyra every night while fairies dance to his song. The infernal roaring sound that can be heard in the cave's inside walls that has inspired the people's imagination is most likely caused by underground water falls and rivers.

Mullein of Crete (Verbascum arcturus) ✍

We cross the torrent, moving up slightly before we take the path down to the little church of Agios Nikolaos.

We pass the torrent once more to find a small gorge

descending on our left. We suddenly find ourselves surrounded by water. Small falls, dimples and streams complete the picture. The coolness of the water is tangible. The magic melody from the running waters is enough to convince the visitor to stop for a while. One can only believe that in these waters nymphs and fairies bathe. Their divine presence is still in the air. Only a few people were lucky enough to have laid eyes on these creatures. (Many years ago Scandinavian girls did not hesitate to jump in the crystal waters!)

False hemp (Datisca cannabina) ℘

Off the pathway, on the banks of the stream that descends from Potistiria grows the false hemp (Datisca Cannabina), an Asian plant, almost identical to the hemp (Cannabis indica), whose cultivation is illegal due to the narcotic substance that can be produced from it.

℘ Rockrose (Cistus creticus)

27

The Church of Agios Nikolaos, 4 km.

A few hundred meters away we come across a clearing. There, we discover the Church of Agios Nikolaos, a small church made of stone, hidden among huge cypress trees that have grown there for centuries. The circumference of their trunk is over 6 meters. Their root goes deep into the ground and allows them to spring in dry and infertile ground without suffering the effects of the summer heat. The great endurance of their wood made was the cause for their extensive use, which began from the antiquity. They were use almost everywhere! In Knossos, Phaestos, Egypt, in the construction of ships...Their excessive use has lead Venice to the decision to forbid the export of the Cretan cypress trees in 1414.

The mountains form a tower over our heads. A small pathway, on our left, leads to Kalyvaki, the building that overlooks the gorge from Xyloskalo to the village of Samaria and a bit further. A place taken out from a fairytale. It is alleged that here laid the ancient town of Keno and Apollo's temple. The truth will remain sealed though. According to Diodoros of Sicily, however, this was the birthplace of Diana Vritomartis. Some pieces of clay vessels and links, an arrow peak and a copper ram that were discovered by chance indicate a temple. Besides the small church on can find a permanent stone guardhouse, which used to be the cheese dairy of Viglides (big family of Samaria) and a stone fountain springing cool water.

29

Cretan peony (Paeonia clusii) ✍

Mullein (Verbascum macrurum) ✍

Dragon arum ⇨
(Dracunculus vulgaris)
and dragon's wort in
left ⇩

In springtime we come across some exceptionally big and beautiful flowers decorating the place. This is the Cretan peony (Paeonia clusii), an endemic plant of Crete. According to mythology, the medicine god Paeon, whose name is mentioned on a clay plaque in Knossos, had used this plant to cure Pluto when Hercules wounded him. It is to that god that it owes its name, Paeonia. At the clearing of the church, the visitor can admire the beauty of other plants: the

mullein (Verbascum macrurum), which has the shape of a big yellow candlestick and of course the huge dark red brown blooms of the Dragon arum (Dracunculus vulgaris).

It is the most impressive plant of the gorge. The visitor must pay extra attention though! Its poison is so dangerous that no animal touches it. On an east Cretan sarcophagus we find the dragon arum as an ornamental motive (found in the Archaeological Museum of Heraklion). Ancient Greeks used to associate these peculiar plants to snakes, representing the secrets of Hades.

The altitude is at 500m and our pathway continues to reach the spring **Vrysi, 5 km**, it passes over the torrent and keeps going. Incredible mountains

surround us, the forest is everywhere and the river with the huge round rocks, the beautiful small waterfalls and the crystal ponds runs under our feet. Next we come across another **new spring**. Although, we do not know its name, we welcome its fresh water.

☞ The distances are signposted like this

Have a look, on your left, you discover that the mountain has subsided and revealed a mountainous valley and a new gorge, Kalokampos. The proud peaks of Mavri and Melidaou rise in the background. The ruins of an old castle can be seen closer to us, on our right as we scan the gorge. A smaller gorge is formed in front of us, vertically to the path. It is called Sidiropoulo.

On the top of the hill, opposite the gorge, lies the **chapel of Agios Georgios** with its eternal soul mate, a marvelous cypress tree. The Hora or Kryptes, the place where the residents of the ancient Tarra and Samaria used to hide their treasures lies a bit further on. The passage which leads up there is so narrow that two people can't cross it walking side to side and thus it provides the ideal shelter for the treasure.

We then descent towards the bed of Sidiropoulo. The

Similar signs are found in all leisure spots and give valuable information

area is called Kolardachtis, **6th km.** And the visitor can still make out many strongholds, remains of the island's Turkish occupation. A small surprise awaits for us at the bed of the small gorge: thousands of stones, big and small, are placed there by the visitors who wanted to leave their trace on the area, creating thus small pyramids, small "belfries".

The bed of the torrent is dry. The water has disappeared in the sand. It will appear in Kefalovrysia, under the plane trees of the great spring.

A walk of one kilometer under the hot sun, the sand, pebbles and rocks and we reach the settlement of Samaria.

The village of Samaria, 7 km

Instinct or need, the truth remains that we cross the wooden bridge which connects the torrent's banks, at a fast pace, in order to rest in the shadow of the mulberry trees and the fig trees around the two spouts which never stop pouring water. This is the best place if one wishes to have a snack.

Around us, nothing but ruins. Most of the houses are whitewashed, with arches and upper floors but there are also one-storied houses made of stone without the slightest decoration like the cheese dairy of the mountains. They remind us ages lost in time...

In the past the village, built at 300m altitude, was full of life. Even though the people were isolated from the outside world, especially in wintertime, they did their best to use their resources as to live a good life.

Their main occupations were:

Cattle raising. Their cattle used to browse mainly in the mountain regions: (Poria, Potistiria, Kallergis, Linoseli.)

Apiculture. They produced fine honey thanks to the pine trees and the numerous honey-producing plants (thyme, savory, spiny savory, marjoram, Jerusalem sage...)

Lumbering. Wood trade was at its peak (there were water powered saws near Agios Nikolaos and after the fountain of Cartridge – Vrysi tis Perdikas) together with the trade of pine tree bark (pitikas) proper for fishing because of its ability to float. Tanners also used it. It also produced resin and charcoal.

There was an olive press.

There was also a water powered system, called "rasotrivi", where wooden hammers used to hit wool to make it longer lasting, almost water proof so as to be used for the construction of the thick

❖ Oil press

shepherd's coarse cloaks, also indispensable to the peasants.

Finally, there laid the famous water mills of Samaria. One has only to close his eyes to picture all the people coming with small sailboats, donkeys and mules from their distant villages to grind their wheat and other cereal! God can only imagine their fatigue!

Hunting was also an indispensable part of their occupations. Most of the men were skilful hunters especially in the hunt of the wild goat (agrimia). References from the ancient years and the medieval times mention the very capable bowmen of Sfakia with a great deal of admiration. " They are excellent users of the bow and their arrows whistle through the air, " mentions the French Jacques le Sage.

According to a distich from Sfakia:

He, who is not brave
and does not know his way with guns
should not reside
in the island of Crete

and it continues:

The people of Sfakia shall live
as long as these mountains will stand
Together with their weapons
that they are very fond of...

38

These people bear the mark of Artemis – Diana, goddess of hunting. They are born bowmen, hunters, brave. The hardships of the mountains and nature, the difficulties and adversities of life have made them capable, adventurous, wild but also hospitable. The times of joy and the feasts were always there:

"The bow bounds over the strings of the lyre, its sharp sound springs out, sometimes dragged, sad and tender and with divine joy. People recite their distiches while others dance the circular folk dances.

The village was abandoned in 1962 after the government's decree to declare the gorge as a "National Park". Only the guardhouse and the worker's house are in good condition. Chania forest inspection service has recently started restoring all the old buildings one by one. Only the olive press, a class room for

other times joyful, merry and lively.

The barrel taps open to fill the glasses with wine and tsikoudia (pure vine spirit). The smell of meat cooked on charcoal appeased the Gods and filled people's hearts teaching and the first floor of the future hospital building have been restored so far.

Five mules are at the traveler's disposal in case of emergency or fatigue. There is also a helicopter landing spot in case of an emergency.

NATIONAL PARK OF SAMARIA
Pathway Map

OMALOS

Mavri
2133m

Melinta
2133m

Kallergis
1680m

Poria

Museum

Kanave △

Xyloskalo
WC

Tourist
Pavilion

Neroutsiko
WC

Xepitiras

Riza tis sikias
WC

Psilafi
2000μ.

Agathopi △

Daimonospilios

Linoseli

Gkigkilos
2085m

△ Prinias

Volakias
2116m

Kalyvaki

Potistiria

Kalokampos

Agios Nikolaos
WC

keno

Vrysi

Nea vrysi
Agios Georgios

Sidiropoulo

Chora

Avlimor
1843m

Samaria
WC

Christos

Osia Maria

Avlimo
1760m

**Vrysi tis
perdikas**

Psirirsta
1485m.

Kefalovrysia

Ma
14

Trypes aera

Kefala
1454m

WC

Metamorfosi

Portes

Kouvara
1186m

Agia Parakevi

Legends
Surface 48,5 km

⌒ Caves

♗ Tower

△ Mountain peak

⚲ Spring

⌘ Settlement

✚ Church

L Antiquities

〰 Path

▬ Limits of the National Park

WC

**Agios
Georgios**

Agia Roumeli (old)

Agia Triada

Agios
Antonios

△ Aggelokar

Venetian
Castle

Tarra

Panagia Kyra

Agia Roumeli (new)

Roman cemetery

Libyan Sea

Dist.	Time	Altitude
Entrance guardian post		
Xyloskalo		
1,7	45´	1236m
Neroutsiko		
1	20´	950m
Riza tis sykias		
1	20´	800m
Agios Nikolaos		
0,8	15´	650m
Vrysi		
1	20´	540m
Nouvelle fontaine.		
2	40´	400m
Samaria		
1	20´	300m
Vrysi tis perdikas		
2,8	50´	250m
Kefalovrysia		
1	20´	200m
Metamorfosi		
0,6	15´	180m
3e porte		
1,4	30´	100m
Guardian post		
2,4	45´	50m
Agia Roumeli		
Exit		
16,7	**5.40´**	**0m**

🌿 Local "ambulance"

If there are not many people or much noise around, we can look around carefully and then we will see an "ibex" an agrimi as it is called in Crete. The guardians feed them with mulberry-tree leaves and forage and some of them seem to slowly become tame being so close to the settlement. It is difficult to forget the charming "bebeka" (baby girl" eating from the hands of the guardian Antonis Skoulas. People say that lately they are more numerous or calmer. At least tree female animals, with at least one baby each will allow you to feed them with your bare hands. So one must not miss the opportunity to take a picture!

The National Park of Samaria is the only place the visitor can see the wild Cretan ibex, Capra aegagrus ssp. cretica Schinz, 1838, as well as in some of the tiny islands on the north of Crete: in Agii Pantes opposite of Agios Nikolaos and in Theodorou opposite of Agia Marina in Chania.

It is the most distinctive animal of the Cretan fauna. It is brown with a black and brown stripe running down its back from its scruff to its tail. Its length reaches 1.30 m. and its height is less than 80 cm. It weights 40 kilos at the very most. It can walk easily even on the hardest rocks and its jump can exceed 10 m!

It mates at the end of October and during the entire November. Some describe it as a ritual. When sunset falls, the male reaches the female in its hiding place and starts throwing small stones with its feet. The noise those stones make is the signal for the mating ceremony. The female now knows that her mate is outside waiting to escort her in their night wedding promenade. The babies shall be born in April, in the middle of spring, when the grass is abundant to help them feed and grow.

Some say that there are only a few dozens left while others estimate that there some 3000 of them. The ibex' greatest enemy is mantakes, parasitic insects which look like ticks which suck the animal's blood while another kind of the parasitic insect goes deep into their scruff and choke the animal (pnigarides).

Besides the parasitic insects, which can decimate whole population in just a short time, the wild goat is also faced with two dangerous enemies. Its newly bourns are easy prey for the wild cat (Felix sylvestris) a strong-bodied fair colored animal with dark spots or stripes which is up to 50 cm long and tends to disappear and the "Vitsila" or golden eagle (Aquila chrysaetos) which is dark-brown colored, its head and scruff being a little lighter colored. Its beak and toes are yellowish; its weak span is of 2,27m. It builds its nest on steep rocks and feeds on little mammals.

Other eagles and vultures with wing span of over 2,5 m. like the rapacious bird (Gyps fulvus) which has a naked neck and the bearded vulture (Gypaetus barbatus) which has a terrifying cry don't attack living animals and they feed on carcasses and bones.

There are also other kinds of animals and birds leaving in the gorge, like the badger (Meles meles), the polecat (Martes foina), the mink (Mustela

⤷ Golden eagle (Aquila chrysaetos)

⤷ Naked vulture (Gyps fulvus)

nivalis), the hare (Lepus europaeus), the partridge (Alectoris chukar) and some kinds of hawks and ravens. During the summer months we meet some passing birds like small swallows (Hirundo daurica?), which can escort you between the passages of the gorge, following the airflow.

⤷ Gypaetus barbatus

Returning to the pathway

Once more we take the pathway leading to the sea. At the settlement's limits along the road which leads to the sea, we can enjoy the sight of two little churches, one on our right, under a rock, is dedicated to **Christ** and the other to our left, just at the slope of the mountain is surrounded by cypress trees, dedicated to **Osia Maria**.

Anyone can reach the church, simply by following the path to the torrents' bed and then walking up again until its small surrounding wall. The centuries have altered its name giving it its present form: **Osia Maria – SiaMaria – Samaria**.

The legend has it that a beautiful blonde girl named Chrysomallousa, decided over a question of honor between the Venetians and a family from Sfakia called Skordilides to devote herself to god wearing a vestment and living under the name of Osia Maria. The church id dated from 1379.

In springtime, one can find many orchids in the abandoned fields. We follow the torrent's bed, cross a small wooden bridge, we move inside the gorge itself, this gigantic cut in the guts of the mountains of Sfakia which allows the waters to escape to the sea. As we keep on walking we come across the **"Vrysi tis Perdikas"**, a spring which gives us the chance to freshen up.

⚘ Bishop's ophrys
(Ophrys episcopalis)

Heldreich's ophrys
(Ophrys heldreichii) ⇨

We cross the 8th km. There are eight different ravines meeting with the main gorge. We make our way under the trees. We descend towards the dried bed of the stream. We pass in front of the old sawmill's bases. We cross narrow passages with vertical inner sides. We arrive at **Halasmena Gremna** (Rotten rocks) (The shift of rocks had formed a lake which was crossed by means of a raft). The pathway seems endless, the fatigue starts to show even more...it is about time we came across some water. Listen to their murmur.

🦤 Geological formation

🦤 Rotten rocks

🦤 Kefalovrysia

We are at the 10th km. The water appears once more under the huge plane trees. It's the big spring, **Kefalovrysi**. Its cool water and its encouraging sound will accompany us until Agia Roumeli. Those who feel thirsty can drink from there without fear. That same water is brought to the village passing through the black pipelines. On the right side of the path we can distinguish water coarse and the ruins of an old watermill. There are about ten of those from the village of Samaria till Agia Roumeli.

Some big stones are deliberately placed in the water to allow us to cross the river dozens of times, without getting wet. Those have been recently replaced by small, wooden, removable footbridge. Some blooming rose-bays (Nerium oleander) add a new color to the already richly colored landscape.

After the settlement of Samaria, the two slopes of the mountains, which converge and deviate like two parallel walls along the whole distance give us the impression that they will meet each other forever trying to block our way through. Indeed, the opening between the two sides gets so narrow that one thinks that the way to the sea is blocked. These narrow spots, these giant natural gates, are called the "Portes" (doors) or Sidiroportes (iron doors).

Sidiroportes, 11 km

We know that the mountain's effort to block the way is in vain: the river's water runs beside our feet murmuring between the stones and the pebbles. These narrow passages, those "Castle-gates" remain impregnable. No matter how many times the Turks tried to conquer them, they failed. In 1770, during the revolution of Daskaloyiannis, Yiannis Bonatos and his 200 brave men resisted vigorously against the Turks and thus saved about 4000 women and children who were persecuted and managed to find shelter in the gorge. In 1867 Omer Pasha disembarked 4000 Turks but he did not manage to enter the gorge.

This was the passage used by King George and the Greek government in their effort to escape in the Middle East, on May 23rd 1941, when Crete was under German occupation. During their occupation, the Germans tried to eliminate the partisans that were hiding in the gorge but they never managed to capture them as the partisans knew all the passages and moved easily among the rough and inaccessible mountains of the region. The confrontations with the enemy did not fear them and they always made the enemy suffer great losses. They thus continued the tradition of the great resistance of Sfakia.

⚘ Cretan symphyandra
(Symphyandra cretica)

53

Here is the kingdom of a great number of chasmophytes. The gorge's guts are covered with them. Even the smallest crevice of the rocks has become a natural flower pot (see photo). Their mere existence seems to be a mystery!

We have reached **the 11th km**, about 200m, before the little **church Metamorfosis**. It is here that we encounter the so called "air holes" which transport hot and cool air as if they were prehistoric monsters trapped in the great depths of the earth. Next comes a large clearing beside the little church. Running waters, tables, benches. We take a short breath before we descend to the riverbed once more and we head straight to the third and most impressive door of all.

🌸 Bell flower (Campanula laciniata)

🌸 Scorpion Vetch of Crete (Coronilla globosa)

⇦ Staechelina
petiolata

We are at the 12 km. We now cross a narrow passage, which does not exceed three meters in width. The rock's sides become vertical rising up to 300 m. over our heads. The stone's side is naked and smooth. For millions of years have licked and smoothed the rocks. Our soul is overwhelmed by awe. The sunrays can hardly penetrate the bottom of the passage. A pleasant coolness rests on our face. The wind seems to come from nowhere. The games of the light

are unique. We are filled with awe. We stand speechless! If one happens to cross the gorge in the early summer one becomes witness of a strange yet amusing phenomenon. The wind uproots the fennels (Ferrulago thyrsifolia?) that fall from the sky like parachutes. Sometimes you may here them land on your feet making a "pluff" sound. The wind or the kri kris might also force a small stone over the edge that echoes in the gorge's walls. One must be extra careful!

Returning to the real world

After passing the third gate the gorge broadens. We abandon the world of fairies and supernatural beings and we direct towards the world of "the common people". The sea is in the air. We taste it at every breeze.

The water of the gorge has dug a deep ditch inside the rock and flows on our right and left. It is here that we come across the famous dittany (Origanum dictamus) and other interesting therapeutic plants.

The Cretan dittany, called dictamnos, erontas or stomatohorto by the natives is an aromatic perennial plant known all over the world. It decorates rock crevices to 1600 cm of altitude. This healing plant is one of the miracles herbs, which were used by Ancient Greeks. Hippocrates, Theophrastus and Dioskorides mention them all. Aristotle mentions that when the wild goats get hurt by some arrow, they eat or chew dittany and they use it heal their wound.

Many are these who were killed in their attempt to pick up this miraculous plant from the rocks. It is lucky that some people decided to cultivate it in Emparos. They

 Dittany (Origanum dictamnus)

60

🕭 Guardian's house at the exit

even export abroad.

Two kilometers separate us from the old village of Agia Roumeli, which abandoned as well. Its inhabitants have searched for a better life elsewhere. In 1954, during a flood, a violent wave has swept away most of the houses built on the torrent's left side.

The old village of Agia Roumeli

At the entrance of the village, **at the 14th km**, next to the guard house we find some hastily erected canteens (or some old houses adapted to the canteens), which offer refreshments and souvenirs. This is our final stop. We cross the village.

61

On our right, among the ruins, a small road leads to the Church of Agios Georgios. We cross some typical houses and we reach the exit of the village. A colorful arched bridge made of stone strides the torrent. A fig tree (Ficus carica) on his right and an Indian fig tree (Opuntia ficus indica) on his left seem to guard it. An intervention in the area has recently destroyed the Indian fig tree.

A few steps from there, we encounter the picturesque little church of Agia Triada and on the opposite side, in the distance, the little church of Agios Antonios. It is, in fact, a cave properly adapted to church.

We come to end of our journey. The road is covered with concrete and is easy to walk as long as our feet are not covered with blisters. We

cross the river for the last time passing over a bridge made of concrete, revealing lack of taste. Right next to it, another bridge is being built to help the cars to reach Agia Triada. We now enter the new village of Agia Roumeli, built on the ruins of Ancient Tarra. This town has prospered during the Roman Period in such degree that it had minted its own coin bearing the Cretan ibex and arrow on one side and a bee on the other. On our left, we can see the ruins of the roman cemetery.

The name Agia Roumeli comes from the Arabic words for water (aia) and Greece (Roumeli) and means Greek water. It may also be associated with the roman goddess Rumilia according to Dephner.

On our left the riverbed has swallowed enormously. In the middle of the bed, between stones and pebbles, we find two little bridges showing a not so distant past when people, horses, donkeys and flocks used it to cross the river. Nowadays nobody uses them. Only the seabirds sit on the stone railing to get some rest and observe the people from a distance!

The new village of Agia Roumeli

At the village's entrance we are welcomed by the **Church of Panagia Kyra.** This is the exact place, where the Doriens had built a temple dedicated to god Apollo in the 5th century B.C. It is said that Apollo hid himself there after Python's death to escape from his father's wrath. According to Pausanias he fell in love with the nymph Akakalida whom he saw rising from the blue sea and blinded with passion, he forgot his duty and that day the sun did not rise until very late in the day. Even to this day the sunrays do not reach the gorge until noon. The ruins of the temple and certain mosaic works can be still seen.

We are surrounded by oleanders (Nerium Oleander) and osiers (Vitex agnus-castex). In late spring the place is filled with a plant bearing beautiful rosy and dark blue violet blooms. It is called Larkspur (Delphinium staphisagria). During that same period, we come across a plant called Horehound (Ballota acetabulosa) famous for its calices, which were used for wicks in church oil lamps and in night lamps.

❧ Osiers (Vitex agnus-castus)

✿ Lice bane, larkspur
(Delphinium staphisagria)

✿ Horehound (Ballota acetabulosa)

We have walked 16 km total. Our journey has reached its end. The beach waits for a nice swim. No doubt that we deserve it. On the right of the small deck the sand is incredible and the waters crystal clear. For those wishing to fill their batteries the taverns are the best choice

Ы Chora Sfakion

Those leaving from Agia Roumeli right away to Hora Sfakion or Palaiochora should be careful not to miss their boat. The others can choose between a hotel room and a nice spot under the pine trees near the river. There they can open their sleeping bags or put up their tents. Rest easy! The Venetian castle[1] built on the

mountain above, watches over you while you sleep.

If you are ready for new

Я Palaiochora

adventures and you want to follow the path leading to Anopolis or Loutro, be sure that the journey will be just as exciting. An hour and a half walk from the beach the path leads to an enormous beach with great sand and pine trees and springs of potable water in the sand itself. A beautiful church built in the 10th century, dedicated to Agios Pavlos, makes this beach serene and imposing beyond words.

⚓ Loutro

1. In reality it is a Turk Castle. The Turks used the Byzantine technique in communications. They used bright signals to send the information they needed from castle to castle. That is also the reason they built their castles on tops. In Agia Roumeli there are four castles, two on the west, over the village and two in the east of the gorge, in the area Aggelokampi, which can be accessed from the gorge of Elygia. One of them is clearly visible but the other three can only be seen from a close distance

⚓ Aradena

General information

Transportation to Samaria:
- Through tourist agencies
- By bus from Chania
- Nea Katastimata square Tel. 2821093306 and 28201091228

The return by boat from Agia Roumeli to the Hora Sfakion and Palaiochora

	Tel.
Chania:	2821044822
Agia Roumeli :	2825091221
Police department of Hora Sfakion:	2825091205
Port Authority of Hora Sfakion:	2825091292
Port Authority of Palaiochora:	2823041214
Forrest Authority Xyloskalo:	2821067179
Chania:	2821092287
Samaria:	2825091276
Agia Roumeli:	2825091254
Greek mountaineering Club :	2821044647
and	2821044359

Medical care: *Agia Roumeli* in the summer months, *Samaria* in the summer months, *Anopolis*, all twelve months, *Chora Sfakion*, all twelve months, *Palaiochora*, all twelve months

---

Works of the same author :

- *The Orchids of Crete and Karpathos, Heraklion 1998*
- *Herbs, Aromatic plants and Edible plants of Crete (coming out soon)*
- *Follow us in Spinalonga (coming out soon)*

Bibliography

1. Alibertis Antonis
   The Orchids of Crete and Carpathos
   Heraklion 1998
2. Alibertis Antonis
   The Gorge of Samaria and its plants
   Heraklion 1994
3. Psilakis Nikos
   The gorge of Samaria
   Minotaurus Publications, Heraklion
4. Michalis Toumbis
   The Gorge of Samaria, Yesterday and today
   Athens 1994
5. Giannoukos Iatridis
   The Gorge of Samaria,
   Athens 1985
6. Zacharis A.
   The Gorge of Samaria
   Periigitis Publications, Athens